U.S. WARS

THE SPANISH-AMERICAN WAR

A MyReportLinks.com Book

Carl R. Green

MyReportLinks.com Books

 an imprint of
Enslow Publishers, Inc. **E**
Box 398, 40 Industrial Road
Berkeley Heights, NJ 07922
USA

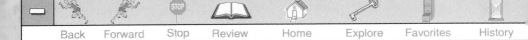
MyReportLinks.com Books, an imprint of Enslow Publishers, Inc.

Library of Congress Cataloging-in-Publication Data

Green, Carl R.
    The Spanish-American War / Carl R. Green.
        p. cm. — (U.S. wars)
    Includes bibliographical references (p.) and index.
    Summary: Discusses how the interests of American expansionists in the
Spanish colony of Cuba eventually resulted in a war with Spain.
    ISBN 0-7660-5091-2
    1. Spanish-American War, 1898—Juvenile literature. [1. Spanish-American
War, 1898.] I. Title. II. Series.
E715 .G74 2002
973.8'9—dc21

                                2001008195

Printed in the United States of America

10 9 8 7 6 5 4 3 2 1

To Our Readers:
Through the purchase of this book, you and your library gain access to the Report Links that specifically back
up this book.
The Publisher will provide access to the Report Links that back up this book and will keep these Report Links
up to date on **www.myreportlinks.com** for three years from the book's first publication date.
We have done our best to make sure all Internet addresses in this book were active and appropriate when we
went to press. However, the author and the Publisher have no control over, and assume no liability for, the
material available on those Internet sites or on other Web sites they may link to.
The usage of the MyReportLinks.com Books Web site is subject to the terms and conditions stated on the
Usage Policy Statement on **www.myreportlinks.com**.
In the future, a password may be required to access the Report Links that back up this book. The password
is found on the bottom of page 4 of this book.
Any comments or suggestions can be sent by e-mail to comments@myreportlinks.com or to the address on
the back cover.

Photo Credits: © Corel Corporation, pp. 1 (background), 3; Courtesy of Arlington National
Cemetery, p. 42; Courtesy of Historical Collections & Services of the Health Sciences Library,
University of Virginia, p. 41; Courtesy of MyReportLinks.com Books, p. 4; Courtesy of PBS: Crucible
of Empire, p. 21; Courtesy of PBS: Remember the Maine, p. 11; Courtesy of Small Planet
Communications, Inc., pp. 16, 37; Courtesy of SocialStudiesHelp.com, p. 14; Courtesy of The New
York Public Library, p. 19; Courtesy of The Spanish-American War Centennial Web site, pp. 12, 33;
Courtesy of Theodore Roosevelt Association, pp. 27, 35; Courtesy of Thinkquest Library, p. 18;
Courtesy of U.S. Naval Historical Center, pp. 24, 25; Enslow Publishers, Inc., pp. 22, 29; Kansas State
Historical Society, p. 1; Library of Congress, p. 31.

Cover Photo: Kansas State Historical Society

Cover Description: Buffalo Soldiers fighting in Cuba

Contents

MyReportLinks.com Books
Great Books, Great Links, Great for Research!

MyReportLinks.com Books present the information you need to learn about your report subject. In addition, they show you where to go on the Internet for more information. The pre-evaluated Report Links that back up this book are kept up to date on **www.myreportlinks.com**. With the purchase of a MyReportLinks.com Books title, you and your library gain access to the Report Links that specifically back up that book. The Report Links save hours of research time and link to dozens—even hundreds—of Web sites, source documents, and photos related to your report topic.

Please see "To Our Readers" on the Copyright page for important information about this book, the MyReportLinks.com Books Web site, and the Report Links that back up this book.

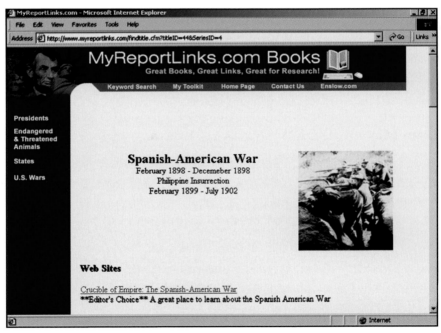

Access:

The Publisher will provide access to the Report Links that back up this book and will try to keep these Report Links up to date on our Web site for three years from the book's first publication date. Please enter **ASA1416** if asked for a password.

> The Internet sites described below can be accessed at
> **http://www.myreportlinks.com**

▶ **Crucible of Empire: The Spanish-American War** *EDITOR'S CHOICE
This multimedia site provides comprehensive information about the
Spanish-American War, including a time line, newspaper headlines,
popular sheet music from the time, and a quiz.

Link to this Internet site from http://www.myreportlinks.com

▶ **USS *Maine*: Remember the *Maine*** *EDITOR'S CHOICE
This site examines the history of the USS *Maine*, and discusses two
recent investigations that tried to uncover the cause of the explosion
that sank the battleship.

Link to this Internet site from http://www.myreportlinks.com

▶ **The Spanish-American War Centennial Web Site** *EDITOR'S CHOICE
This site includes plenty of information about the war, including weapons
and ship profiles, firsthand accounts of the fighting, and the role of
journalists during the war. It also organizes events into categories such as
"War in Cuba," "War in the Philippines," and "War in Puerto Rico."

Link to this Internet site from http://www.myreportlinks.com

▶ **William McKinley and the Spanish-American War** *EDITOR'S CHOICE
This site contains information about the Battle of Santiago, in which
only one American sailor was killed. You will also find many political
cartoons from the time, and a link to a page devoted to the presidency
of William McKinley.

Link to this Internet site from http://www.myreportlinks.com

▶ **The Spanish-American War in the Philippines (1898)** *EDITOR'S CHOICE
This PBS Web site explores the Spanish-American War in the
Philippines. Here you will learn about the war's key military figures
and their accomplishments.

Link to this Internet site from http://www.myreportlinks.com

▶ **Rough Rider Colonel Roosevelt** *EDITOR'S CHOICE
At this Web site you will find a history of Theodore Roosevelt and
the Rough Riders. Here you will learn how the Rough Riders earned
their name, along with an account of the well-known Battle at San
Juan Heights.

Link to this Internet site from http://www.myreportlinks.com

Report Links

▶**American History and Government**
This site answers basic questions about the Spanish-American War.
Here you will learn about the causes of the war, the nature of imperialism, and
some of the war's key players. You will also find a collection of newspaper
headlines and political cartoons.

Link to this Internet site from http://www.myreportlinks.com

▶**Arlington National Cemetery**
A monument to the Spanish-American War was erected at Arlington National
Cemetery in 1902. This site describes the history and provides a picture of
the monument.

Link to this Internet site from http://www.myreportlinks.com

▶**The Battle of Manila Bay**
This site provides a firsthand account of the Battle of Manila Bay as written
by Admiral George Dewey. Look for the famous quote, "You may fire when
ready, Gridley."

Link to this Internet site from http://www.myreportlinks.com

▶**Biography of Theodore Roosevelt**
After serving with distinction in the Spanish-American War, Theodore
Roosevelt went on to become the youngest United States president up to that
time. This site describes both his personal and presidential accomplishments.

Link to this Internet site from http://www.myreportlinks.com

▶**The Cuban Experience**
This site contains a brief summary of the Spanish-American War and has links
to the history of Cuba, its culture, and the Cuban War for Independence.

Link to this Internet site from http://www.myreportlinks.com

▶**Effects of the Press on Spanish-American Relations in 1898**
This site contains an essay that incorporates newspaper articles and cartoons
from the time of the war. It shows how the media helped shape American
public opinion and the direction the country was to take.

Link to this Internet site from http://www.myreportlinks.com

Report Links

 The Internet sites described below can be accessed at
http://www.myreportlinks.com

▶ **Historical Museum of Southern Florida**
This site presents interesting information about the role that Florida
played in the war. You will find information such as how the army
built a fort to protect Miami from the Spanish navy.

Link to this Internet site from http://www.myreportlinks.com

▶ **National Museum of Health and Medicine:**
Spanish-American War
The National Museum of Health and Medicine Web site contains
information about the army hospitals, medical personnel, and the
battle they waged against disease during the Spanish-American War.

Link to this Internet site from http://www.myreportlinks.com

▶ **Naval Historical Center Events—Spanish-American War**
This site has many photographs and images of the USS *Maine* and
other United States battleships that were deployed during the war. It
also includes information about Spanish warships.

Link to this Internet site from http://www.myreportlinks.com

▶ **New York Public Library: A War in Perspective,**
1898–1998
This site contains a chronology of war events and discusses public
debates that took place during the Spanish-American War. Also
included are interesting propaganda cartoons.

Link to this Internet site from http://www.myreportlinks.com

▶ **Philippine History Time Line**
This time line has links to a summary of the Spanish-American War
and a biography of Emilio Aguinaldo.

Link to this Internet site from http://www.myreportlinks.com

▶ **The Rough Riders**
At this Web site you will learn about Theodore Roosevelt and his
role in the Spanish-American War. It includes Roosevelt's book,
The Rough Riders. You can also use the search engine to find specific
people or events.

Link to this Internet site from http://www.myreportlinks.com

		STOP					
Back	Forward	Stop	Review	Home	Explore	Favorites	History

Report Links

The Internet sites described below can be accessed at
http://www.myreportlinks.com

▶**Sailors, Soldiers, and Marines of the Spanish-American War**
This site contains statistical information and historic records of the people
who served in the army, navy, and marines during the Spanish-American War.

Link to this Internet site from http://www.myreportlinks.com

▶**The Spanish-American War**
This information-packed site includes lots of details about Cuba, the USS
Maine, and "yellow journalism." You will also find photos, maps, and film
clips about the Spanish-American War.

Link to this Internet site from http://www.myreportlinks.com

▶**Spanish-American War**
This site offers a brief informative description of the Spanish-American War. It
is organized into sections that include causes of the war, events, and results.

Link to this Internet site from http://www.myreportlinks.com

▶**Spanish-American War: America's War**
This site has simple and clear descriptions detailing the history of the war. The
information is broken down chronologically. It begins with the sinking of the
USS *Maine* and ends with the capture of Manila.

Link to this Internet site from http://www.myreportlinks.com

▶**Spanish-American War Medal of Honor Recipients**
This site spotlights African-American medal recipients and details the brave
actions that distinguished these soldiers during the Spanish-American War.

Link to this Internet site from http://www.myreportlinks.com

▶**The Spanish-American War in Motion Pictures**
At this Library of Congress Web site you will find movie clips of the
Spanish-American War. The topics include the Rough Riders and
the USS *Maine*.

Link to this Internet site from http://www.myreportlinks.com

Report Links

The Internet sites described below can be accessed at
http://www.myreportlinks.com

▶ **Spanish-American War in U.S. Media Culture**
This site provides an essay about the images of the war in American
media and includes stills and short clips from early films.

Link to this Internet site from http://www.myreportlinks.com

▶ **Theodore Roosevelt**
America's Story from America's Library, a Library of Congress Web site,
provides information about Theodore Roosevelt, the Rough Riders,
and an interesting story about the teddy bear.

Link to this Internet site from http://www.myreportlinks.com

▶ **William McKinley: The Imperialist President**
At this Web site you will learn about the events that prompted William
McKinley to declare war on Spain. You will also learn about McKinley's
other foreign policy decisions.

Link to this Internet site from http://www.myreportlinks.com

▶ **The World of 1898: The Spanish-American War**
This site highlights many of the key figures in the war, such as
Theodore Roosevelt, Commodore Dewey, and Spanish General
Weyler. You will also find period photographs, and links to maps
and indexes.

Link to this Internet site from http://www.myreportlinks.com

▶ **Yellow Fever and the Reed Commission**
This site is devoted to the doctors, scientists, and military personnel
who proved that yellow fever was caused by mosquitoes, not by direct
contact with infected people. Learn about the history of yellow fever
and its connection to the Spanish-American War.

Link to this Internet site from http://www.myreportlinks.com

▶ **1898–1998: Centennial of the Spanish-American War**
This site contains a brief history of the war, along with photos and
quotations. It also provides a useful history of relations between Cuba
and the United States.

Link to this Internet site from http://www.myreportlinks.com

Spanish-American War Casualties

Note: The following battle casualties are for 1898, and include losses suffered in Cuba, Puerto Rico, and the Philippines. USS *Maine* and Philippine Insurrection casualties are listed separately, as are deaths from disease. Spanish casualties are estimates and include losses suffered during the 1895–98 campaign to subdue Cuban rebels.[1]

United States of America	Spain
Total American Casualties, 1898 • **332** Killed • **1,641** wounded • **2,957** died from disease	**Total Spanish casualties, 1895–1898** • **5,500** killed • wounded (number not known) • **49,500** died from disease
USS Maine *explodes (February 15, 1898)* United States: 202 killed, 51 wounded	
Manila Bay, Philippines (May 1, 1898) United States: 1 killed, 8 wounded	Spain: 167 killed, 214 wounded
El Caney, Puerto Rico (July 1, 1898) United States: 81 killed, 360 wounded	Spain: 235 killed or wounded, 120 captured
San Juan Heights, Cuba (July 1, 1898) United States: 205 killed, 1,180 wounded	Spain: 215 killed, 370 wounded
Philippine Insurrection (1899–1902) United States: 4,200 killed, 2,800 wounded	Filipino insurgents: 20,000 casualties

▶ A Brief Time Line

1898—*Feb. 15:* The USS *Maine* explodes in Havana harbor.

—*March 8:* Congress approves "Fifty-Million-Dollar Bill" to rebuild military.

—*April 21:* U.S. Navy blockades Cuban ports.

—*April 25:* U.S. Congress declares a state of war against Spain.

—*May 1:* Battle of Manila Bay in the Philippines.

—*July 1:* Battles of El Caney and San Juan Heights in Cuba.

—*July 3:* United States fleet destroys Spanish squadron outside Santiago harbor.

—*Dec. 10:* Treaty of Paris signed by United States and Spain: Cuba granted independence; Puerto Rico and Guam become United States territories, and Spain is given $20 million for the Philippines.

1899—*Feb. 4:* Philippine Insurrection begins.

1902—*May:* Cuba finally granted independence; United States maintains a military base at Guantanamo Bay.

—*July 4:* End of the Philippine Insurrection.

Remember the *Maine!*

Captain Charles Sigsbee was proud of his ship. The USS *Maine* was one of the U.S. Navy's newest warships. Manned by a crew of 22 officers and 328 sailors, the gleaming white battleship looked unsinkable.

The *Maine* lay anchored at Key West, Florida, as the calendar turned to January 1898. Sigsbee's thoughts often

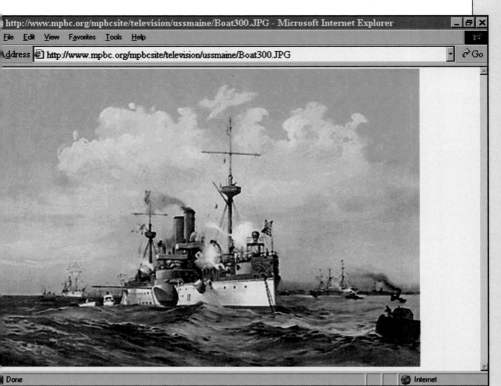

```
http://www.mpbc.org/mpbcsite/television/ussmaine/Boat300.JPG - Microsoft Internet Explorer  _ 8 X
File  Edit  View  Favorites  Tools  Help
Address  http://www.mpbc.org/mpbcsite/television/ussmaine/Boat300.JPG           Go
```

▲ The USS Maine *exploded in the harbor of Havana, Cuba, in February 1898. The United States blamed Spain and declared war in April 1898.*

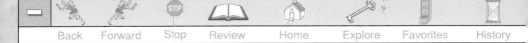

turned to the troubled island of Cuba, just ninety miles away. The Cuban people were fighting to rid themselves of Spanish rule. Fitzhugh Lee, the American consul general, had warned that American lives and property were at risk. As a safeguard, the War Department put the *Maine* on high alert.

▶ Showing the Colors

On January 24, 1898, Sigsbee received his orders. It was time, President William McKinley said, to "show the colors." A visit by the battleship would serve a triple

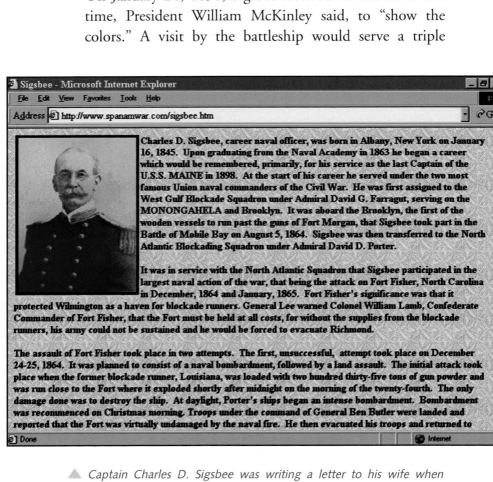

Charles D. Sigsbee, career naval officer, was born in Albany, New York on January 16, 1845. Upon graduating from the Naval Academy in 1863 he began a career which would be remembered, primarily, for his service as the last Captain of the U.S.S. MAINE in 1898. At the start of his career he served under the two most famous Union naval commanders of the Civil War. He was first assigned to the West Gulf Blockade Squadron under Admiral David G. Farragut, serving on the MONONGAHELA and Brooklyn. It was aboard the Brooklyn, the first of the wooden vessels to run past the guns of Fort Morgan, that Sigsbee took part in the Battle of Mobile Bay on August 5, 1864. Sigsbee was then transferred to the North Atlantic Blockading Squadron under Admiral David D. Porter.

It was in service with the North Atlantic Squadron that Sigsbee participated in the largest naval action of the war, that being the attack on Fort Fisher, North Carolina in December, 1864 and January, 1865. Fort Fisher's significance was that it protected Wilmington as a haven for blockade runners. General Lee warned Colonel William Lamb, Confederate Commander of Fort Fisher, that the Fort must be held at all costs, for without the supplies from the blockade runners, his army could not be sustained and he would be forced to evacuate Richmond.

The assault of Fort Fisher took place in two attempts. The first, unsuccessful, attempt took place on December 24-25, 1864. It was planned to consist of a naval bombardment, followed by a land assault. The initial attack took place when the former blockade runner, Louisiana, was loaded with two hundred thirty-five tons of gun powder and was run close to the Fort where it exploded shortly after midnight on the morning of the twenty-fourth. The only damage done was to destroy the ship. At daylight, Porter's ships began an intense bombardment. Bombardment was recommenced on Christmas morning. Troops under the command of General Ben Butler were landed and reported that the Fort was virtually undamaged by the naval fire. He then evacuated his troops and returned to

▲ Captain Charles D. Sigsbee was writing a letter to his wife when the USS *Maine* exploded in February 1898. Almost 80 percent of the battleship's crew died on that terrible night.

purpose. First, it would assure Spain that the United States was a friend, not a foe. Second, German warships had been seen in Cuban waters. The presence of a United States warship would warn the Germans to steer clear of Cuba. Finally, if trouble did break out, the *Maine* would be on hand to protect American lives.[1]

The Spanish played by the rules when the *Maine* arrived in Cuban waters and dropped anchor in Havana Harbor. The two navies exchanged salutes, and the governor sent Sigsbee a case of sherry. As a further show of friendship, the American officers were invited to watch a bullfight. The day passed peacefully, despite the anti-American handbills that were handed out. The message urged Spanish loyalists to resist the visit of the "Yankee Pigs."[2]

Sigsbee's crew was on alert. Armed sentries stood guard around the clock. The engine room crew kept the ship's engine ready for action, and the crew practiced "gun-pointing" drills. Escorts stayed close to all Spanish and Cuban visitors. Through all this, Sigsbee played the gracious host. One of his guests was Clara Barton, founder of the American Red Cross. Barton wrote that she watched as the "crew, strong, ruddy and bright, went through their drill for our entertainment."[3]

▶ "A Terrible Mass of Fire"

The night of February 15, 1898, seemed as peaceful as all the others. The bugler blew taps at 9:10 P.M. With sentries posted and most of the crew asleep, Captain Sigsbee sat down to write a letter to his wife. At 9:40 P.M., without warning, an explosion ripped the hull of the great ship apart. Sigsbee later wrote, "It was a bursting, rending, and crashing roar of immense volume, followed by heavy,

ominous metallic sounds. . . . Then there was intense blackness and smoke. The situation could not be mistaken. The *Maine* was blown up and sinking."[4]

As Sigsbee reached the deck, he saw that his ship was sinking, bow first. Fires were burning everywhere. Most of the crew had been trapped in their bunks, and were already dead or dying. Some of them had been blown into the sea, or had jumped from the burning deck. An observer on a nearby ship saw "a terrible mass of fire and explosion, a black mass. Then we heard . . . a cry, 'Help! Lord God save us! Help! Help!'"[5] As Captain Sigsbee prepared to abandon

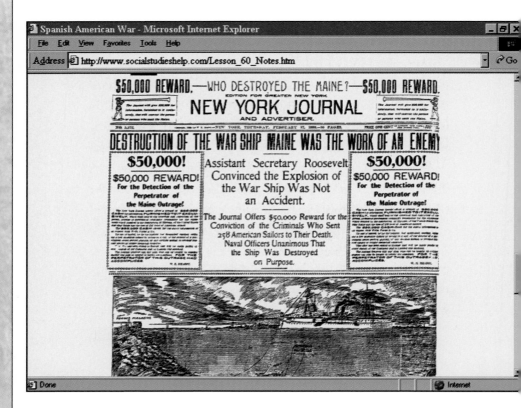

▲ The front page of the February 17, 1898, edition of the New York Journal *declares that the sinking of the USS* Maine *was the work of an enemy.*

ship, boats from nearby ships arrived to aid in the rescue. Many of the sailors pulled from the oily water were beyond help. The casualty list shows that 262 men died that night. Another fifty-one suffered terrible wounds.

Sigsbee cabled news of the sinking to Washington, D.C. President McKinley was shaken by the reports, but refused to panic. He said he would withhold judgment until all the facts were known. By then, American news-papers had hit the streets with their own version of the disaster. *The New York World*'s headline read, USS *MAINE* BLOWN UP IN HAVANA HARBOR. Not to be outdone, the *New York Journal*'s headline screamed, THE WARSHIP *MAINE* WAS SPLIT IN TWO BY AN ENEMY'S SECRET INFERNAL MACHINE.[6]

On March 21, 1898, a naval board of inquiry reported that the *Maine* had been sunk by "a submarine mine." The board went on to say that it could not fix the blame on any person or persons.[7] Theodore Roosevelt, the assistant secretary of the navy, voiced his outrage. "The *Maine* was sunk by an act of dirty treachery by the Spaniards," he wrote. Others argued that a coal fire that spread to an ammunition bunker could have caused the blast.

In the end, the truth did not matter. The country was gripped by a bad case of war fever. Crowds marched in the streets, chanting, "Remember the *Maine*! To hell with Spain!"[8]

The Road to War

The war cries of 1898 were inspired in part by America's hunger for an empire. Factory owners saw colonies as good markets for their products. Expansionists argued in favor of acquiring territory as a means of extending the nation's economic and political influence. American rule, expansionists insisted, would lift native peoples out of

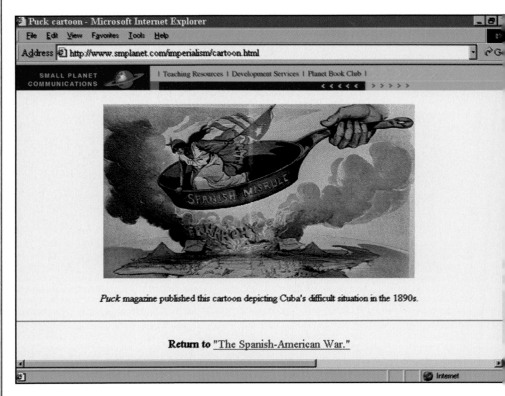

This political cartoon illustrates the difficult situation Cuba faced as a result of Spanish misrule in the 1890s. It shows how corrupt Spanish rule was creating a state of anarchy in Cuba.

poverty and ignorance. According to a nineteenth-century doctrine called "manifest destiny," the United States felt it had the right and duty to expand its territory in North America. John Hay, U.S. ambassador to England, summed up this sense of manifest destiny. In a letter to President McKinley, he wrote: "It is a pity we have so many men among us who do not . . . believe in the American people and in their glorious destiny."[1] Booker T. Washington, an African American, held an opposing view of America's duty. In the *Indianapolis Freeman*, Washington wrote, ". . . the Philippine Islands should be given an opportunity to govern themselves. They will make mistakes but will learn."[2]

▶ Island Rebellion

In the 1890s, the expansionists had their eyes on the island of Cuba. Spain's rich Caribbean colony lay only ninety miles south of Florida. Its rich sugar plantations were greatly prized. Indeed, much of the $50 million invested in Cuba by American businessmen had gone into sugar. Also fueling the expansionists' interest in Cuba was the fact that Cubans were in the midst of a revolution against Spanish rule. Cuban born José Martí, based in New York City, had spearheaded a revolt against Spain in 1895. Ever since, Cuban rebels had waged a guerrilla war. Swift-moving bands ravaged small towns, burned plantations, and tore up rail lines. Pro-Spanish Cubans who fell into their hands were hacked to death with machetes.

To combat the rebels, Spain turned to General Valeriano Weyler. "Mercy has no place in war," the new governor-general said. In 1896, Weyler enforced a policy known as reconcentration (*reconcentrado* in Spanish). At his orders, soldiers forced everyone who lived in the

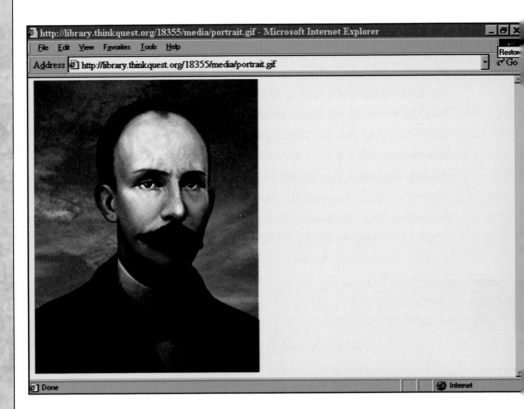

http://library.thinkquest.org/18355/media/portrait.gif - Microsoft Internet Explorer

File   Edit   View   Favorites   Tools   Help

Address http://library.thinkquest.org/18355/media/portrait.gif

Done   Internet

▲ *Cuban political activist José Martí planned a revolt against Spain in 1895, while living in exile in New York City. He died in a skirmish with Spanish troops soon after he returned to Cuba.*

countryside to move into fortified towns. The troops then burned anything that might aid the rebels. Inside the towns, food and shelter were in short supply. In two years, thanks to "Butcher" Weyler, hunger and disease killed 400,000 men, women, and children.[3]

Weyler's ruthless methods slowed the rebellion, but did not end it. Led by General Máximo Gómez, the rebels kept on fighting. In the United States, lurid reports from the island built support for Gómez. People flew Cuban flags and gave money to help the Cuban cause. President McKinley heard the pleas, but McKinley, a veteran of the

Civil War, was slow to respond. "I have been through one war," he said. "I have seen the dead piled up, and I do not want to see another."[4]

McKinley tried to work with Spain through diplomatic channels. At one point there was talk of buying Cuba and Puerto Rico, but Spain's Queen Maria Cristina refused. Spanish honor was at stake, her government said. The nation that had once ruled much of southern North America, including the Caribbean, would not give up her last two colonies there. At a minimum, McKinley said, Spain must replace Weyler with a new governor.

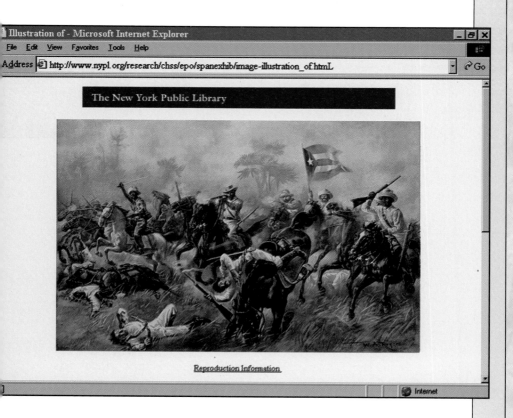

Illustration of - Microsoft Internet Explorer

File   Edit   View   Favorites   Tools   Help

Address   http://www.nypl.org/research/chss/epo/spanexhib/image-illustration_of.htmL   Go

The New York Public Library

Reproduction Information

Internet

The Battle of Desmayo occurred in October 1896. Cuban troops numbering 479 charged a Spanish army of over 2,500. Almost all of the Cubans were killed in this terrible slaughter.

To keep the peace, Spanish officials called Weyler home. His replacement moved quickly to change the harsh policies. Spain also promised to give the Cubans a measure of self-rule. In return for this concession, Spain's ambassador to the United States, Enrique Dupuy de Lôme, asked the United States to cut off the flow of supplies to the rebels. Dupuy then wrote a letter to a friend in which he called McKinley "a low politician" who "[caters] to the rabble."[5] A Cuban spy stole the note and gave it to the *New York Journal*. When it was printed on February 9, 1898, the letter set off a storm of protest.

▶ The Yellow Press

For once, the *Journal* and its rival, the *New York World*, lined up on McKinley's side. On most days, their stories accused him of ignoring Spanish crimes. Critics called newspapers of this type—those that attacked or smeared a person's reputation—"the yellow press." The name referred to the smeary yellow ink used to print the then-popular Yellow Kid cartoon. In their rush to sell papers, owners William Randolph Hearst and Joseph Pulitzer often exaggerated events. When a report came in that a prisoner had drowned, the *Journal* headlined the story, "Feeding Prisoners to Sharks." The *World* took up the challenge. Its next issue described a Cuba with "blood on the roadsides, blood in the fields, blood on the doorsteps, blood, blood, blood!"[6]

All too often, reporters that were sent to Cuba wrote their stories from the comfort of their hotels. Travel was risky, so they tended to use Cubans friendly to the rebels as sources. Those who did venture into the countryside sometimes had trouble finding news about the uprising. The artist Frederic Remington found little to sketch, so he sent

YELLOW JOURNALISM

◄ HOME
RELATED LINKS ▼

Hearst Biography
Davis Biography
Headline Gallery
Cartoon Gallery

The Spanish-American War is often referred to as the first "media war." During the 1890s, journalism that sensationalized—and sometimes even manufactured—dramatic events was a powerful force that helped propel the United States into war with Spain. Led by newspaper owners William Randolph Hearst and Joseph Pulitzer, journalism of the 1890s used melodrama, romance, and hyperbole to sell millions of newspapers--a style that became known as **yellow journalism**.

"Proceed at once to the Philippine Islands. Commence operations against the Spanish fleet. Use utmost

The term yellow journalism came from a popular <u>New York World</u> comic called "Hogan's Alley," which featured a yellow-dressed character named the "the yellow kid." Determined to compete with

WILLIAM RANDOLPH HEARST

THE FILM
TIMELINE
YELLOW JOURNALISM
1890s MUSIC
RESOURCES
VISITORS' FORUM
SITE MAP

Internet

▲ *The Spanish-American War is often referred to as the first media war. Two newspaper owners, William Randolph Hearst and Joseph Pulitzer, are most commonly associated with the term* yellow journalism. *They never let the facts stand in the way of telling a story that would boost the sale of papers.*

a message to Hearst. "There is no war," his cable read. "Request to be recalled."

Hearst fired back a reply that summed up the style of the yellow press. "Please remain," Hearst's cable said. "You furnish the pictures, I'll furnish the war."[7]

Chapter 3 ▶ A Nation Prepares for Battle

The *World* and *Journal* were selling close to 2 million papers a day by 1898. Each report of Cuban victims of Spanish misrule built support for the United States to use force in Cuba. In the end, the loss of the *Maine* tipped the balance. The news of the tragedy completed the change in the nation's outlook. A few years before, most Americans would have jeered at the call to fight a foreign war.

A few critics tried to protest. Some recalled the dark days of the Civil War, which had cost some 600,000 lives. Others argued that the United States should not meddle in

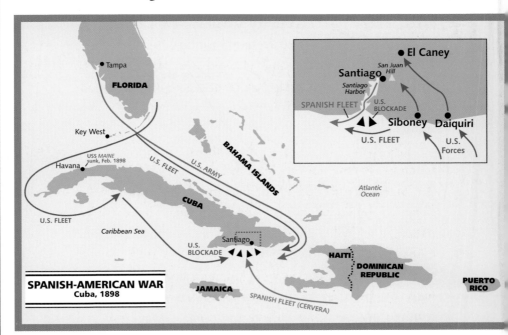

▲ This map shows the ship movement and battles of the Spanish-American War in and around Cuba.

the affairs of other countries. Their cries were lost in a rising tide of manifest destiny. It was our duty, preachers and politicians said, to pick up "the white man's burden." Their zeal helped create a desire to share the American way of life with "backward" countries.[1]

War Declared

President McKinley still hoped for peace—but the public wanted war. Even the nation's women were up in arms. A headline in the *World* declared, AMERICAN WOMEN READY TO GIVE UP HUSBANDS, SONS, AND SWEETHEARTS TO DEFEND THE NATION'S HONOR.[2] Reports from Madrid did little to reduce tensions. Ambassador Woodford wrote, "[Government officials] prefer the chances of war, with the certain loss of Cuba, to the overthrow of the [monarchy]."[3]

McKinley bowed to the pressure. In early March, he asked Congress to pass the "Fifty-Million-Dollar Bill." The law gave him $50 million to spend for defense. The action stunned the Spanish and cheered the Cuban rebels. McKinley then went a step further and demanded freedom for Cuba. Spain asked for more time—but there was no time.

On April 11, 1898, a worn-down McKinley asked Congress for the power to use military force. He spoke of the "horrible miseries" of the Cuban people and the harm done to American trade. Congress began its work by passing the Teller Amendment. The act promised that Cubans would be free to govern themselves after the war. Between sessions, the sound of singing floated through the halls of the Capitol building. One favorite song was inspired by an army marching tune. "Hang General Weyler to a sour apple tree, as we go marching on," the members sang.[4]

Congress passed a joint resolution on April 19. It authorized the president to "use the entire land and naval forces of the United States" to free Cuba. McKinley signed the document a day later, and on April 21, sent the North Atlantic Squadron under Admiral William Sampson to Havana to set up a blockade. Spain issued a declaration of war on April 23. On April 25, Congress officially declared war on Spain. The declaration was dated April 21 in order to justify Sampson's blockade of Cuba. At home, a Kansas newspaper noted, "everywhere in this good, fair land flags were flying."[5] The nation was at war with Spain.

The newly-commissioned USS Oregon was one of the battleships that took part in the naval blockade of Cuba.

▶ Preparing to Fight

Declaring war was the easy first step. Getting ready to fight was a more challenging task. The War Department's use of the $50 million approved in March points to one weakness. The navy grabbed $34 million, leaving the army with only $16 million.[6] This lopsided split of the funds spoke to the era's belief in strong navies. Navy officials used their money to order massive supplies of coal, powder, and shells. Agents hurried to buy yachts and freighters that could be turned into warships. The navy's newest battleship, the *Oregon*, was called home from the West Coast.

The army shared the navy's zest for combat, but not its readiness. The regular army could muster only 28,000 officers and foot soldiers. On April 23, McKinley put out a call for 125,000 volunteers. Young men rushed to the recruiting offices—and found chaos waiting. The army lacked modern guns, smokeless powder, wagons, tents, and uniforms. Of the $16 million it received in March, the War Department

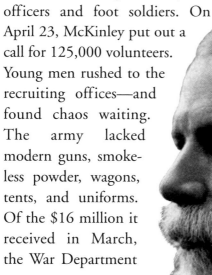

Secretary of War ▶
Russell A. Alger.

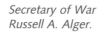

spent most of the money on coastal defense. Secretary of War Russell A. Alger seemed unaware of the army's pitiful state. Given ten days, he promised McKinley, the army could put 40,000 men in Cuba. Even Alger must have known this was a foolish vow.[7]

Cheers turned to panic as rumors spread that a Spanish fleet was heading for the East Coast of the United States. In Boston, shop owners rushed to move their goods inland. A Georgia congressman pleaded with the navy to guard Jekyll Island, which lay off the Georgia coast. Some millionaires, he explained, had their winter homes there. Teddy Roosevelt did what he could to boost morale. Although it was no match for a modern warship, he anchored a Civil War ironclad near one coastal city.[8]

▶ Teddy's Rough Riders

The army scrambled to equip and train its eager volunteers. At first, officials stuck to policies written for a peacetime army. Recruits were issued winter uniforms, even though Cuba was a tropical island. Smokeless powder was scorned as too new and untested. Buying horses required that sellers be given thirty days notice. One bureaucrat was upset by the order to speed things up that Roosevelt waved at him. "Oh, dear!" the man sighed. "I had this office running in such good shape—and then along came the war and upset everything!"[9]

Roosevelt left the War Department and joined an elite volunteer force. The "Rough Riders" were picked for their skills as "horsemen and marksmen." Some were cowboys and lawmen. Others were veterans of the wars with American Indians. A few were wealthy sportsmen who played polo. Citing his lack of "military work," Roosevelt signed on as second in command to Colonel Leonard Wood.

The Rough Riders and Colonel Roosevelt by The Theodore Roosevelt Association - Microsoft Internet E...

File   Edit   View   Favorites   Tools   Help

Address http://www.theodoreroosevelt.org/life/Rough_Riders.htm   Go

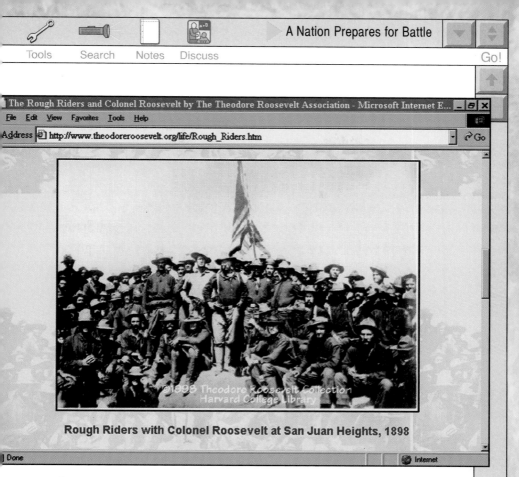

Rough Riders with Colonel Roosevelt at San Juan Heights, 1898

Done   Internet

▲ *Roosevelt and his troops, nicknamed the Rough Riders, fought in the Battle of San Juan Heights on July 1, 1898. They were known for their courage, daring, and high spirits.*

The Rough Riders unit trained in the heat and dust of San Antonio, Texas. Roosevelt drilled his troops on foot and on horseback. When he became too friendly with the men, Wood reined him in with a sharp lecture. For their part, the Rough Riders admired the man they called "Teddy." They were a rowdy lot, but they worked hard to become good soldiers.

At the end of May 1898, the Rough Riders boarded a train for Florida. By then, the navy had fought the first great battle of the Spanish-American War.

Chapter 4

"You May Fire When Ready"

The orders that led to the Battle of Manila Bay were dated June 1897. If war broke out, the War Department wanted to blockade Spain's colonial naval bases. In Cuba, that meant keeping ships from entering or leaving Havana Harbor. Far out in the Pacific Ocean, the target was Manila Harbor in the Philippines.

Most Americans knew the tale of Spanish misrule in Cuba. The Philippines were more of a riddle. As one humorist put it, no one knew whether the Philippines "were islands or canned goods."[1] The newspapers had given little space to the plight of the Filipino people. If they had, the stories would have been similar to those coming out of Cuba. Spain exploited the people and the natural resources of the Philippine Islands. In 1896, angry Filipinos had revolted against Spanish rule.

▶ Commodore George Dewey

The job of blockading Manila Harbor fell to Commodore George Dewey. Theodore Roosevelt had picked Dewey for the Asian command. "I've looked in [Dewey's] eyes," he explained. "He's a fighter."[2] A veteran of the Civil War, Dewey had helped lead the effort to rebuild the navy. Even his critics admired his courage and seamanship.

As war drew near, Dewey prepared his seven-ship squadron for battle. He filled his bunkers with coal and ordered fresh stores of powder and shells. Work crews scraped the hulls and rigged armor for the gunners. To camouflage his gleaming white ships, Dewey ordered his sailors to repaint them a dull gray. Next, the men tossed overboard everything made of wood. In battle, enemy shells could turn wooden chests, chairs, and tables into sprays of deadly splinters.

On April 26, 1898, Dewey sailed for the Philippines. His mission was to capture or destroy the Spanish fleet in the Pacific. As the American ships left Hong Kong, British sailors, who understood the advantage Manila's fortified harbor gave to the Spanish Fleet, wished the Americans a safe voyage. "A fine set of fellows," they told each other. "Unhappily, we shall never see them [alive] again."[3] Commodore Dewey and his men had other ideas.

▶ Battle of Manila Bay

On May 1, in predawn darkness, the USS *Olympia* led the squadron into Manila Bay. With only their stern lights showing, the ships slipped past two Spanish forts. At the last moment, a lookout spotted the intruders. One of the forts opened fire. American gunners returned the fire and quickly silenced the guns. A few hours later, Dewey found the Spanish fleet anchored at the Cavite naval base.

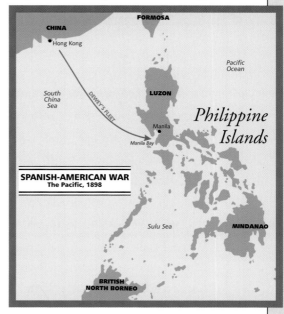

▲ Commodore George Dewey's fleet sailed from Hong Kong to Manila Bay in the Philippine Islands.

Admiral Patricio Montojo had chosen to fight there, sheltered by his shore guns. The Spanish had more ships than the Americans, but Dewey had more firepower.

The Spanish opened the battle with a wild salvo as all their guns fired at once. The American ships held their fire as they plowed through a curtain of bursting shells. At 5:41 A.M., Dewey calmly told the *Olympia's* captain, "You may fire when ready, Gridley."[4] The squadron's eight-inch guns roared and roared again. Clouds of smoke and black powder filled the turrets. In the engine rooms, men fainted in 150-degree heat.

The American shells slammed into their targets. On the Spanish ship *Cristina*, a shell exploded in the sickbay, killing doctors and wounded alike. By 7:35 A.M., the Spanish guns had fallen silent. Three of Montojo's ships were in flames. Dewey pulled his squadron back to check his powder stores and to feed his men. At 11:00 A.M., he sent the *Petrel* to shell the last shore batteries. Soon afterward, the Spanish ran up a white flag. Faced with the threat of bombardment, Manila's garrison also surrendered.

The victory was complete. The Spanish lost their entire fleet, along with 381 men killed and wounded. None of Dewey's ships suffered major damage. Only eight men had been wounded, all on the *Baltimore*. The only American death was caused by heatstroke.[5]

▶ A Nation Celebrates, the Fighting Continues

Word of Dewey's triumph reached the United States on May 7, 1898. The news sent crowds into the streets to celebrate. McKinley promoted the new hero to rear admiral. Cities hurried to name schools and streets in Dewey's honor. At night, families gathered around their pianos to sing the hit song, "How Did Dewey Do It?" Merchants printed Dewey's picture on buttons, hats, beer mugs, and soap wrappers.[6]

In the Philippines, the war dragged on. The Spanish had lost their naval fleet, but their army troops still held the islands' strong points. Dewey attacked the problem on two fronts. First, he asked Washington to send soldiers for an assault on Manila. Then, he landed a fiery rebel leader behind Spanish lines. Emilio Aguinaldo had been fighting the Spanish since 1896. Armed with rifles seized in an earlier skirmish, his ragged army swept through the countryside. The Spanish stayed holed up in Manila and waited.

http://lcweb.loc.gov/rr/hispanic/1898/img/aguinaldo.jpg - Microsoft Internet Explorer

File Edit View Favorites Tools Help

Address http://lcweb.loc.gov/rr/hispanic/1898/img/aguinaldo.jpg   Go

Done   Internet

Emilio Aguinaldo was a leader in the fight for Philippine independence. In 1898, he led a Filipino army against Spain during the Spanish-American War.

By August 13, Admiral Dewey had 18,000 American infantrymen on hand and felt ready to take the offensive. After a brief exchange of fire that satisfied Spanish honor, the troops advanced toward Manila. When they entered the city, Spanish General Firmin Jaudenes surrendered. He trusted the Americans to treat his men well. The Filipinos, he feared, had old scores to settle. If they had taken the city, they would likely have killed any Spanish soldiers they captured.

Aguinaldo tried to lead his men into the city of Manila and establish control, but American troops turned him away. Aguinaldo felt betrayed—and with good reason. McKinley had resolved to add the Philippines to America's new empire. He later explained, "[The Filipinos] were unfit for self-government . . . there was nothing left for us to do but to take them all, and to . . . uplift and civilize and Christianize them."[7] What McKinley could not foresee was the depth of Aguinaldo's rage. On January 6, 1899, the rebels launched a ferocious guerrilla war against their new ruler—the United States.

The Battle for Cuba

Back home, the Fifth Army Corps was training in makeshift camps near Tampa, Florida. General Nelson Miles, a tough old Civil War veteran, was in command. General William Shafter served as his field commander. At six-feet tall, and weighing three hundred pounds. Shafter "looked like two men rolled into one."[1] Along with

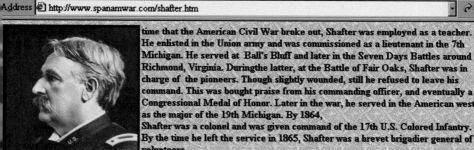

shafter - Microsoft Internet Explorer

File   Edit   View   Favorites   Tools   Help

Address http://www.spanamwar.com/shafter.htm   Go

time that the American Civil War broke out, Shafter was employed as a teacher. He enlisted in the Union army and was commissioned as a lieutenant in the 7th Michigan. He served at Ball's Bluff and later in the Seven Days Battles around Richmond, Virginia. During the latter, at the Battle of Fair Oaks, Shafter was in charge of the pioneers. Though slightly wounded, still he refused to leave his command. This was bought praise from his commanding officer, and eventually a Congressional Medal of Honor. Later in the war, he served in the American west as the major of the 19th Michigan. By 1864, Shafter was a colonel and was given command of the 17th U.S. Colored Infantry. By the time he left the service in 1865, Shafter was a brevet brigadier general of volunteers.

In 1867, William Shafter re-entered the military, securing a post as a lieutenant colonel in the regular army, eventually serving with the 24th U.S. Infantry on the frontier. In the post-Civil War army, promotion was slow. Shafter retained this position for ten years, from 1869 until 1879. In 1879, Shafter was promoted to full colonel, and placed in command of the 1st U.S. Infantry, and stayed with this command from 1879 until 1897. In the latter year, Shafter was finally promoted to brigadier general. The new rank brought a new command. This time, Shafter was placed in command of the Department of California.

With the outbreak of the Spanish American War, Shafter was appointed a major general of volunteers and assigned to the Fifth Corps, being organized in Tampa, Florida. One reason for his selection was his apparent lack of political ambitions. The Fifth Corps consisted mainly of U.S. regulars, though there were some volunteers, such as the 71st New York, and the "Rough Riders." By this time, Shafter, at age 63, was a corpulent three hundred pounds in weight and suffering from the gout. He was no condition to command troops in either Florida or in the

Done   Internet

▲ *Major General William Shafter commanded United States land forces in Cuba during the Spanish-American War. Despite falling ill during the campaign, he was credited with the capture of Santiago.*

his fellow officers, he lacked the experience needed to mount an invasion of Cuba.

Freight cars stacked up on sidings around Tampa, their contents a mystery. Soldiers sweated under the Florida sun and cursed their wool uniforms. For supper they ate "embalmed beef"—canned meat that tasted as bad as it smelled.[2] One colonel complained that a third of his men had never fired a gun. Theodore Roosevelt looked at the jumble of troops, horses, and equipment and shuddered. "Tampa was a scene of the wildest confusion," he wrote. "There was no semblance of order."[3]

▶ Guantanamo Bay

General Miles planned a fall invasion, hoping to avoid the summer yellow fever season. Early in May, the Spanish navy spoiled his timetable. Leading a squadron of six warships, Admiral Pascual Cervera left Spain and headed for Cuba. His mission was to break the blockade that was strangling the island. Instead, the U.S. Navy managed to trap him in Cuba's Santiago harbor. The news forced Miles to act quickly. If Cervera escaped, his ships would be free to attack the invasion fleet.

Six hundred and fifty marines landed at Guantanamo Bay, Cuba, on June 10, 1898. Their job was to set up a coaling station for the navy. With the aid of Cuban rebels, the landing went smoothly. The real battle started when the marines hit the main Spanish lines. In the firefight that followed, it was the Spanish defenders who broke and ran. The First Marine Division had won the war's first land action.

Rumors of Spanish warships on the prowl kept the main invasion force in port in Florida. When the all clear came on June 14, forty-eight transports sailed for Cuba.

The soldiers were packed into airless holds. Fresh food was in short supply. Spirits were high, but turmoil was the order of the day. Roosevelt grumbled, ". . . one transport [carried] guns, and another had the locks for the guns. Soldiers went here, provisions went there . . ."[4]

Despite the confusion, the army managed to land 17,000 troops in the Daiquiri-Siboney area of Cuba. Roosevelt's Rough Riders and the other infantry troops saw action for the first time in a small skirmish at Las Guasimas on June 24. The battle began when hidden riflemen opened fire on the Rough Riders. Men fell all

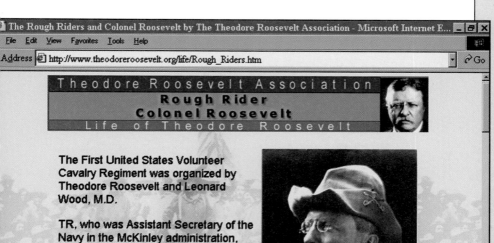

The Rough Riders and Colonel Roosevelt by The Theodore Roosevelt Association - Microsoft Internet E...

File   Edit   View   Favorites   Tools   Help

Address   http://www.theodoreroosevelt.org/life/Rough_Riders.htm   Go

Theodore Roosevelt Association
Rough Rider
Colonel Roosevelt
Life of Theodore Roosevelt

The First United States Volunteer Cavalry Regiment was organized by Theodore Roosevelt and Leonard Wood, M.D.

TR, who was Assistant Secretary of the Navy in the McKinley administration, and a leading advocate of the liberation of Cuba, the Spanish colony then fighting for its independence, asked the Department of War permission to raise a regiment after Spain declared war on the United States on April 24, 1898. Wood, an army doctor who had won the Medal of Honor fighting the Apaches in the 1880s, was President William McKinley's physician, and a close friend

Done   Internet

▲ *Theodore Roosevelt served as commander of the courageous Rough Riders during the Spanish-American War. He became a national hero by demonstrating bravery during the Battle of San Juan Heights.*

along the narrow jungle trail as Spanish bullets thudded home. When "Teddy's Terrors" at last spotted their targets, their relentless advance forced the Spanish to retreat. "When we fired a volley," a Spanish prisoner said, "instead of falling back [the Americans] came forward. That is not the way to fight, to come closer at every volley."[5]

▶ Battle of San Juan Heights

A week later, three battles—two on land and one at sea—sealed Spain's fate in Cuba. By this time General Shafter was stretched out on his cot, felled by the heat. The land battles began on July 1, 1898, at the village of El Caney. Backed up by artillery fire, the soldiers charged the village. This time the defenders held their ground. The battle raged on until the Spanish ran low on bullets and had to withdraw. It was a costly victory for the Americans, who suffered 441 casualties. The Spanish lost 235 men; another 120 surrendered.[6]

The main battle took place along a ridge anchored by Kettle Hill and San Juan Hill. Two American divisions came under heavy fire as they approached the ridge. A Spanish observation balloon that floated above the troops told the Spanish gunners where to aim. The hard-pressed American soldiers cheered when a shell fragment collapsed the balloon. With Shafter ill, no orders were coming through. Pinned down at the foot of the two hills, field officers took matters into their own hands.

At Kettle Hill, the Rough Riders rallied behind Colonel Roosevelt. Two African-American units, the Ninth and Tenth Cavalry, joined them. Roosevelt, his glasses glinting in the sun, ordered an attack. As he spurred his horse forward, his men cheered and hurried after him. Each time a man fell, another rushed in to take his place.

Tools   Search   Notes   Discuss   Go!

The wild charge broke the Spanish lines. The defenders fled, leaving the Rough Riders in control of Kettle Hill.

A matching story unfolded on San Juan Hill. There, Lieutenant Jules Ord yelled, "Come on you men! We can't stay here! Follow me!"[7] Hundreds of soldiers grabbed their rifles and surged up the hill behind him. Behind them, three rapid-firing Gatling guns opened up. The hail of bullets forced the Spanish defenders to keep their heads down. The mad assault broke through barbed wire fences and spilled into the Spanish lines. In the hand-to-hand fighting that cleared the trenches, Lieutenant Ord was one of the first to die.

Battle of Santiago de Cuba - Microsoft Internet Explorer

File Edit View Favorites Tools Help

Address http://smplanet.com/imperialism/santiago.html   Go

SMALL PLANET COMMUNICATIONS | Teaching Resources | Development Services | Planet Book Club |

Done   Internet

▲ *The Battle of Santiago de Cuba was one of the decisive battles in the Spanish-American War. The "big turkey shoot" destroyed a Spanish fleet and helped secure Cuba's independence from Spain.*

▶ "A Big Turkey Shoot"

The Americans rested, regrouped, and drove the Spanish from a second set of hills. The new lines looked down on the roofs of the city of Santiago. The sight inspired the American troops, but supplies were running low. When a general talked about falling back, Roosevelt pointed toward the city. "If we have to move out of here at all I should be inclined to make the rush in the right direction," he said.[8]

On July 3, 1898, the U.S. Navy matched the army's victories. The day began as Admiral Cervera and his squadron tried to slip out of Santiago Harbor. As the six ships turned westward to evade the blockade, they were spotted by American lookouts. The big guns of Admiral Winfield Scott Schley's battleships zeroed in on the fleeing cruisers. By late afternoon all of Cervera's ships were out of action. A seaman on the USS *Oregon* described the battle as a "big turkey shoot."[9]

The crushing defeats sealed Spain's fate in Cuba. Two weeks later, General José Toral surrendered the city of Santiago to General Shafter. The five-week campaign to free Cuba was over.

Chapter 6

Birth of a World Power

The Spanish-American War ended with a rush. American troops followed up the capture of Santiago by landing on the island of Puerto Rico eight days later. The invasion force quickly crushed the island's defenses. The Spanish government, reeling from defeats on land and sea, asked for peace on July 26. Queen Maria Cristina agreed to McKinley's terms, and the two sides signed a truce on August 12, 1898.

From his post in London, John Hay wrote to Theodore Roosevelt. "It's been a splendid little war," he boasted.[1] Soldiers who fought in Cuba would have argued the point. They had slept in jungle mud, sweated in tropical heat, and eaten spoiled food. They had watched their friends suffer and die. Some had died quickly, of wounds suffered in battle. Most had died slowly, of malaria, typhoid, or yellow fever.

The "splendid little war" was costly to both sides. During 1898, American casualties numbered 332 killed, 1,641 wounded, and 2,957 dead from disease. For the years 1895–98, Spanish casualties totaled 5,500 killed and 49,500 dead from disease.

▶ Treaty of Paris

Delegations from the United States and Spain signed the Treaty of Paris on December 10, 1898. The Spanish delegates gave up Cuba, Puerto Rico, and Guam. They wanted to keep the Philippines, but McKinley had his

mind made up. In the end, the United States broke the deadlock by paying $20 million for the islands. The treaty went to the Senate, where it needed a two-thirds vote. When the clerk called the roll, it squeaked through with only one vote to spare, 57–27.[2]

In the space of a single year, the United States had become a world power. Its military strength had been proven against a world power. It had acquired territories in the Pacific and the Caribbean.

Cuba went on to become an independent country in 1902, after three years of United States military rule. Guam and Puerto Rico became United States territories. In 1952, Puerto Rico was raised to the status of a U.S. Commonwealth.

Out in the Philippines, Emilio Aguinaldo called for Filipinos to resist their new masters. The guerrilla war that followed was marked by ambushes, booby traps, torture, and the burning of huts. As casualties mounted, the U.S. Army tried to isolate the rebels by herding villagers into concentration camps. Spain's General Weyler had used the tactic in Cuba and it had backfired. It failed for the United States in the Philippines as well.

The team of General Arthur MacArthur and William Howard Taft finally crushed the rebellion. MacArthur sent "flying columns" into the countryside to track down and destroy the rebels. Taft, in his role as governor-general, won the people's trust by building schools and improving health care. The end came in March 1901, when a task force found Aguinaldo's hiding place and captured him. The rebel leader, his cause lost, asked his people to accept American rule.[3] On July 4, 1902, President Roosevelt officially declared an end to the Philippine Insurrection.

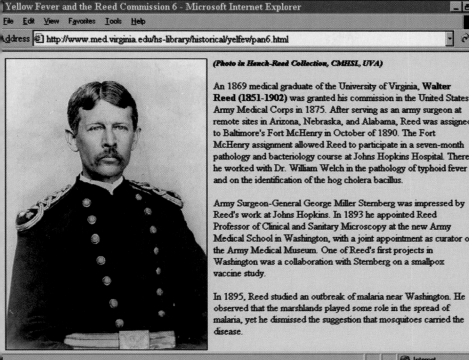

Yellow Fever and the Reed Commission 6 - Microsoft Internet Explorer

File Edit View Favorites Tools Help

Address http://www.med.virginia.edu/hs-library/historical/yelfev/pan6.html Go

(Photo in Hench-Reed Collection, CMHSL, UVA)

An 1869 medical graduate of the University of Virginia, **Walter Reed (1851-1902)** was granted his commission in the United States Army Medical Corps in 1875. After serving as an army surgeon at remote sites in Arizona, Nebraska, and Alabama, Reed was assigned to Baltimore's Fort McHenry in October of 1890. The Fort McHenry assignment allowed Reed to participate in a seven-month pathology and bacteriology course at Johns Hopkins Hospital. There he worked with Dr. William Welch in the pathology of typhoid fever and on the identification of the hog cholera bacillus.

Army Surgeon-General George Miller Sternberg was impressed by Reed's work at Johns Hopkins. In 1893 he appointed Reed Professor of Clinical and Sanitary Microscopy at the new Army Medical School in Washington, with a joint appointment as curator of the Army Medical Museum. One of Reed's first projects in Washington was a collaboration with Sternberg on a smallpox vaccine study.

In 1895, Reed studied an outbreak of malaria near Washington. He observed that the marshlands played some role in the spread of malaria, yet he dismissed the suggestion that mosquitoes carried the disease.

Internet

▲ *Major Walter Reed was a medical officer who helped discover that mosquitoes carry the virus that causes yellow fever.*

The United States ruled the islands until 1949, when the Philippines became an independent nation.

▶ Conquest of Yellow Fever

Back in Cuba, Major Walter Reed was waging a battle against yellow fever. During the war, more soldiers had died of the disease than were killed by Spanish bullets.[4] Reed's first task when he reached Cuba in 1901 was to find the cause. Most doctors thought that victims "caught" yellow fever from contact with someone already infected.

A Cuban doctor named Carlos Finlay disagreed. He said the disease was carried by a mosquito called *Aëdes aegypti*.

Reed and his fellow doctors tested both theories. Volunteers slept in the beds of men who had died from yellow fever. After twenty nights, none of them were sick. To test Finlay's theory, twenty-four volunteers allowed themselves to be bitten by *Aëdes* mosquitoes. Dr. Jesse Lazear fell ill—and died. Others caught the fever, but survived. Nurse Clara Maass was one of them. A few months later she again offered herself as a volunteer. This time Maass died from the disease. In 1976, the U.S. Postal Service issued a stamp in her honor.[5]

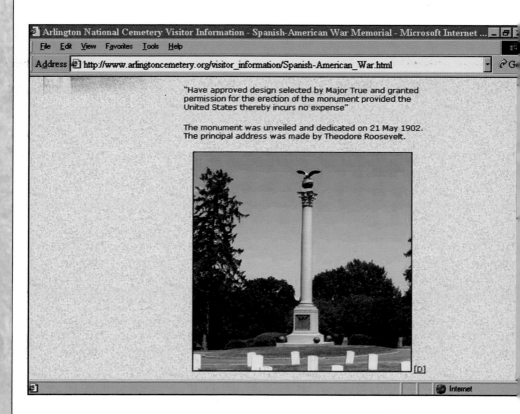

▲ A memorial was dedicated in Arlington National Cemetery on May 21, 1902, to commemorate the brave Americans who died in the war.

Reed showed his proof to Colonel William Gorgas, the army's sanitation officer. The message was clear: mosquitoes carry the virus that causes yellow fever. Gorgas sent out teams to rid Havana of the puddles and pools where the mosquitoes laid their eggs. In a short time the city was free of yellow fever. Gorgas later used the same technique to protect the workers who built the Panama Canal.

Dawn of a New Era

"Teddy" Roosevelt returned home to a hero's welcome. New York promptly elected him as its governor. In 1900, McKinley picked him to be vice president in his successful run for a second term. Many Republican politicians were upset by the choice. As Mark Hanna observed, "Don't any of you realize that there's only one life between that madman and the Presidency?"[6] A year later, when an assassin shot McKinley, the "madman" took his place.

As president, Roosevelt led a nation where technology was changing the way people lived and worked. Automobiles were chugging down city streets. In 1903, the Wright brothers made the first heavier-than-air flight at Kitty Hawk. People talked on telephones and watched the first "moving pictures."[7]

Most Americans welcomed what they believed would be a century of peace and plenty. Few stopped to worry about the evils of city slums, racial injustice, and child labor. After all, this was the nation that freed Cuba and won an empire! No one could have foretold the conflicts and challenges that lay ahead.

Spanish-American War Facts

1. Patrick McSherry, "Casualties During the Spanish American War," *The Spanish American War Centennial Website*, n.d., http://www.spanamwar.com/casualties.htm (September 6, 2001).

Chapter 1. Remember the *Maine*!

1. Allan Keller, *The Spanish-American War: A Compact History* (New York: Hawthorn Books, 1969), p. 32.

2. David Traxel, *1898: The Birth of the American Century* (New York: Alfred Knopf, 1998), p. 99.

3. Ibid., p. 100.

4. "The Spanish-American War: Remember the *Maine*," *An Outline History of the United States*, n.d., http://www.smplanet.com/imperialism/remember.html (September 6, 2001).

5. Traxel, p. 103.

6. Charles H. Brown, *The Correspondents' War: Journalists in the Spanish-American War* (New York: Charles Scribner's Sons, 1967), pp. 120, 123.

7. Traxel, p. 119.

8. Bernard A. Weisberger, ed., *Reaching for Empire, Vol. 8: 1890–1901* (New York: Time Inc., 1964), p. 132.

Chapter 2. The Road to War

1. H. Paul Jeffers, *Colonel Roosevelt: Theodore Roosevelt Goes to War, 1897–1898* (New York: John Wiley & Sons, 1996), p. 18.

2. Janette Thomas Greenwood, *The Gilded Age: A History in Documents* (New York: Oxford University Press, 2000), p. 168.

3. G. J. A. O'Toole, *The Spanish War: An American Epic—1898* (New York: W. W. Norton & Company, 1984), pp. 56–58.

4. David Traxel, *1898: The Birth of the American Century* (New York: Alfred Knopf, 1998), p. 107.

5. Ibid., pp. 98–99.

6. Bernard A. Weisberger, ed., *Reaching for Empire, Vol. 8: 1890–1901* (New York: Time Inc., 1964), p. 130–131.

7. Donald Barr Chidsey, *The Spanish-American War: A Behind-the-Scenes Account of the War in Cuba* (New York: Crown Publishers, 1971), p. 44.

Chapter 3. A Nation Prepares for Battle

1. Patrick McSherry, "The Spanish American War—One American's View," *The Spanish American War Centennial Website*, n.d., http://www.spanamwar.com/Americanview.htm (September 6, 2001).

2. John Baker, *Effects of the Press on Spanish-American Relations in 1898*, n.d., http://www.humboldt.edu/~jcb10/spanwar.shtml (September 6, 2001).

3. David Traxel, *1898: The Birth of the American Century* (New York: Alfred Knopf, 1998), p. 115.

4. Ibid., p. 122.

5. H. Paul Jeffers, *Colonel Roosevelt: Theodore Roosevelt Goes to War, 1897–1898* (New York: John Wiley & Sons, 1996), pp. 134, 136.

6. Donald Barr Chidsey, *The Spanish-American War: A Behind-the-Scenes Account of the War in Cuba* (New York: Crown Publishers, 1971), p. 50.

7. Ibid., p. 83.

8. Traxel, pp. 124–125.

9. Jeffers, p. 157.

Chapter 4. "You May Fire When Ready"

1. Bernard A. Weisberger, ed., *Reaching for Empire, Vol. 8: 1890–1901* (New York: Time Inc., 1964), p. 133.

2. David Traxel, *1898: The Birth of the American Century* (New York: Alfred Knopf, 1998), p. 127.

3. Albert Marrin, *The Spanish-American War* (New York: Atheneum, 1991), p. 46.

4. Ibid., p. 53.

5. Jack Cameron Dierks, *A Leap to Arms: The Cuban Campaign of 1898* (Philadelphia, Pa.: J. B. Lippincott, 1970), p. 52.

6. Marrin, pp. 58–59.

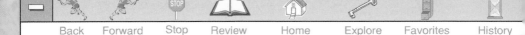
7. Weisberger, p. 139.

Chapter 5. The Battle for Cuba

1. Albert Marrin, *The Spanish-American War* (New York: Atheneum, 1991), p. 78.

2. Ibid., p. 90.

3. "The Spanish-American War: A Splendid Little War," *An Outline History of the United States*, n.d., http://www.smplanet.com/imperialism/splendid.html (September 6, 2001).

4. Ibid.

5. Marrin, p. 101.

6. Donald Barr Chidsey, *The Spanish-American War: A Behind-the-Scenes Account of the War in Cuba* (New York: Crown Publishers, 1971), p. 132.

7. Marrin, p. 109.

8. David Traxel, *1898: The Birth of the American Century* (New York: Alfred Knopf, 1998), p. 198.

9. "The Spanish-American War: A Splendid Little War."

Chapter 6. Birth of a World Power

1. "The Spanish-American War: A Splendid Little War," *An Outline History of the United States*, n.d., http://www.smplanet.com/imperialism/splendid.html (September 6, 2001).

2. Donald Barr Chidsey, *The Spanish-American War: A Behind-the-Scenes Account of the War in Cuba* (New York: Crown Publishers, 1971), p. 152.

3. Albert Marrin, *The Spanish-American War* (New York: Atheneum, 1991), pp. 161–162.

4. "Major Walter Reed, Medical Corps, U.S. Army," *Walter Reed Health Care System*, n.d., http://www.wramc.amedd.army.mil/welcome/history/ (October 2, 2001).

5. "1976 Inductee, Clara Louise Maass, 1876–1901," *The Hall of Fame Inductees*, n.d., http://www.nursingworld.org/hof/maascl.htm (May 15, 2001).

6. Bernard A. Weisberger, ed., *Reaching for Empire, Vol. 8: 1890–1901* (New York: Time Inc., 1964), p. 150.

7. Ibid., pp. 152–153.

Further Reading

Bachrach, Deborah. *The Spanish-American War.* San Diego, Calif.: Lucent Books, 1991.

Brown, Charles H. *The Correspondents' War: Journalists in the Spanish-American War.* New York: Charles Scribner's Sons, 1967.

Carter, Alden R. *The Spanish-American War.* New York: Franklin Watts, 1992.

Chidsey, Donald Barr. *The Spanish-American War: A Behind-the-Scenes Account of the War in Cuba.* New York: Crown Publishers, Inc., 1971.

Dierks, Jack Cameron. *A Leap to Arms: The Cuban Campaign of 1898.* Philadelphia, Pa.: J. B. Lippincott Company, 1970.

Green, Carl R. and William R. Sanford. *The Spanish-American War Soldier at San Juan Hill.* Mankato, Minn.: Capstone Press, 1991.

Jeffers, H. Paul. *Colonel Roosevelt: Theodore Roosevelt Goes to War, 1897–1898.* New York: John Wiley & Sons, 1996.

Marrin, Albert. *The Spanish-American War.* New York: Atheneum, 1991.

Reeder, Colonel Red. *The Story of the Spanish-American War.* New York: Meredith Press, 1966.

Schueler, Donald G. *Theodore Roosevelt.* Berkeley Heights, N.J.: MyReportLinks.com Books, 2002.

Traxel, David. 1898: *The Birth of the American Century.* New York: Alfred Knopf, 1998.